ROAD SCATTER

ROAD

Also by Sandra Meek

Biogeography

Deep Travel: Contemporary American Poets Abroad (editor)

Burn

Nomadic Foundations

SCATTER

poems

SANDRA MEEK

A Karen & Michael Braziller Book

PERSEA BOOKS / NEW YORK

Persea Books, Inc.
277 Broadway
New York, NY 10007

Library of Congress Cataloging-in-Publication Data

Meek, Sandra.
Road scatter : poems / Sandra Meek.—1st ed.
     p. cm.
"A Karen & Michael Braziller book."
ISBN 978-0-89255-419-5 (original trade pbk. : alk. paper)
I. Title.
PS3613.E3325R63 2012
811'.6—dc23

                         2012010957

First edition
Printed in the United States of America
Designed by Rita Lascaro

ACKNOWLEDGMENTS

Deepest thanks to the editors of the following publications in which these poems, some in slightly different versions, first appeared:

American Letters & Commentary: "Road Scatter"
The American Poetry Review: "In case, since you left, you've been wondering,"
Atlanta Review: "Museum of the Party"
Barely South Review: "Circulation," "Still Life with Mouse Torso and Miniature Grand Piano"
Bellevue Literary Review: "Air Hunger"
Catch Up: "Cumulative Sentence"
Cerise Press: "An Elegiac Tone Predominates," "Denial Machine," "Falling Rock"
Connotations Press: An Online Artifact: "Shadow Portrait" and "New Year"
Crazyhorse: "Live Performance"
Green Mountains Review: "Urban Warfare as Design," "O"
The Iowa Review: "The History of Air, Part I"
The Massachusetts Review: "Spreading Ash"
Mid-American Review: "Clearing the House"
Poet Lore: "Swimming at the Y"
Prairie Schooner: "Chemo Session Six," "The History of Air, Part II," "Round Trip"
Quarterly West: "Trapeze," "Wind Event"
The Southern Review: "Columba livia," "Fifteen to Twenty," "Last Rites"
Subtropics: "Moth Season"

"Extinction," "Colony of Ice," "Marble Figure, Descending Panorama," "Healing by Secondary Intention," "New Construction," and "On Vengeance" featured on *Web Conjunctions*' "New Year's Poetry Festival," January 2009.

Special thanks to *Atlanta Review* editors Dan Veach and Memye Curtis Tucker for nominating "Museum of the Party" for a Pushcart Prize.

For my mother

TABLE OF CONTENTS

SHADOW PORTRAIT

Garden pond, a brimming socket.
One gold carp, sautered star.

Icy threads of December light

the last commas of her hair, the few
grayed leaves left tagging
the walkingstick bush a spider has spanned
with dawn silver, cursive stringing

letter to letter in quartertone slide.

The body is a jar of air and lace;
the heart, a ruby beaker a hummingbird sips
all summer from.

What pools and stills is her face, darkened
to flash the sheet

of paper tacked
to brick: shadow all that saves her
from pure outline, charcoal glove

I trace her to—
there, where the light ends.

Columba Livia

The year we understood *city* by *feral*, honeysuckle
smothered so much of spring: the wings' soft slapping, like laundered sheets
flapping on lines tightroping alleys, and from the ledge,
from the orange bead of an eye, the park statue
a steel seed; invisible the little bowls of poison
city elders gift them for fouling chalky white the founding
father bronzed to horse in
heroic gesture, hooves paused midair
corroding. When the seventeenth century darkened
with lost cousins, *passengers* the sky descending
into ripening corn three days transformed
to sweet meat, they ate all winter, the settlers. Each bullet an eye
closing. A field
clear-cut with light. That was history. Then
the farms moved inland until the frontier was desert
skewered with outsized windmills, spinning tridents
scissoring errant wings. Back home, what might be called *country*,
we call them *doves*: *rock*
to distinguish from *mourning*. Cities
are identical and distant, linked by *feral* who settle concrete cliffs
in treeless streets. No two birds marked
the same, *feral* like *snowflake*, a single destination
for drift, for all those shifting continental plates, wing feathers mapped
cinnamon and brick and smoke gray. Only the collar
in common, translucent wine stain
of amethyst and emerald, a strip of sunset forest still glossing
the ashen city air.

The History of Air, Part I

Once there was a *once*, a story
she added each night to
until the calendar slipped
from the wall, her blood running

away from my hand's small pressure
stroking her hand, spilling back
like grape juice down a straw
a child plays, not
drinking—

       Her room's fluorescence
bays the dark beyond
the doorknob she could turn,
once, when constellations glittered
until she clicked them
off behind blinds underscoring
the night she no longer

distinguishes from morning.
She could field
any midnight's lightning,
then, before the question
she'd swept to the back of her brain
wine-stained her skull
with the jewel of a continent

she'd never travel, all
but the purple cap of veins pulling
away from, I swear, the

shrinking bone. I stroke
her hollowing brow; cradle
the ivory knob topping
her spine's pebbled
bow of smoke, memorizing
the fragrance of her strawberry-yogurt moan

as they turn her, the poise
of the oxygen canister in the corner, its bomb-
like mechanism sealed
off as the room's perpetual machine
purrs on—

      Perfect pitch
lies in the bone, the flute
and whorl of it: the body a tuning fork
struck into sound even as language
abandons her—*We swam over lakes, over big thick strings
of water*—for a stammer

in her wrist; the small hiss
of a dowsing-rod nosepiece
gifting her what she
can no longer take
in, the upstaging
air, a magician's last *poof*
as dry ice pours crematorium smoke
into velvet stage curtains, like clapping
two erasers, all chalk

and muffling, as into the pillow
beneath her I could almost,
almost—

Round Trip

1

Enough, these weekend drives, to hold to the distant
approaching hill, wild-

boar bristled with winter-shed trees and a cell tower
star-pulsed, needle-tipped one

aspirant drop of light. Like the one
that clears each day's syringe of air

bubbles bobbing like balloons
schooled to her wrist that birthday sixty-

five years ago, diaphanous
sapphire globes her mother tied off, her own breath

jeweled inside. Lost sky
of blue milk, her translucent face turned away

by Mylar's metallic *get-well-soon*
withering down her hospital room wall

with the raisiny deflation I never knew the lungs' alveoli
could rubber to.

When the day's needle nestles a last
unshot vein, her fist

opens to a flutter of fingers, ghosts of strings
untangling so all the bright

jostling orbs drift
beyond the retrievable, that brief air

just above the body.

2

Clouds shuffle and reshuffle
over the hill, which five
minutes ago was five
minutes away, now receding
to a later hour's
hesitant dusk, all lanes
of the highway blocked by a wreck's

call and response, cars one
by one turning
off their engines until only a semi's
still snuffling, the quieted cars bracketing the one
missed beat in its engine's

flawed timing. Exhaust
rivers the air, wavering
like the road ahead
misengineered to the hill's
born curve now a granite
apron of spillage dotted with stunted
evergreens and dwarf, bare-
boned trees guerilla-
Christmased with beer cans' golden cylinders and shivery

foil boas; one tree's green
ribboned with CDs, disk after
disk rainbowing late sun
around its own
punched-out heart
as if it were the blank at the bull's-eye

of everything.

3

It matters how you tell it, the version
you're driving: in one, the body
rises, helicopter

lifting into afterimage spun
from two crossed planks oaring the sea
of late afternoon air, traffic

moving on, into the shimmering season
tinseling the hill's twigged
cinnamon and gauze,

its buzz cut of winter
gray as the ashtrays she'd
rinse each night, just

to be sure. Or say midnight
begins with ice; in her hospital room, it's as if we're
inside an eggshell shattering when the rain

glasses over to loop the car-
crash the moment the windshield
sucked in and hailed with milky crystals blunt

as rock candy the driver who couldn't
have known what dim stars his world's sweet light
would press down to.

4

So beginning my
impatient half-hour wait for the wreck

to be shouldered and traffic
waved on across a river braced

by a steel bridge which might enter this story
with the hum of a dragonfly torso

or one rib of the helicopter
lifting from the scene, maybe the same

one I watch from her
seventh-floor window, silver pooling

like mercury to its crossbones as it stalls
over the hospital roof. How far

is the throttle in the throat of one
small, flawed engine

from the flood of white light pouring
upward toward warning's

red star? Blinking the beat of the still
pulsing blood, beat of the drip

of morphine toward the knot of
misfiring cells and my waiting

to hear her, somehow, after days
of her voice whirring ever deeper into her

swamped and sinking chest: *enough*, she'd say,
enough.

MARBLE FIGURE, DESCENDING PANORAMA

It's resisting
gravity that

wears, the hill
going down—
weighted with rain, her

upturned hand pools
erosion, a ladle
dipping away cream.

The body
is equal measures

milk and stone, a small room

divided by string. The sky's
acid what tongues

her face to blur—
a quiver of
minute blades spilled and

feather-floating like the fractured
wings of insects also

freighting this air, twisting
in gleam sharp as broken
bottles embedded

in the city zoo's walls.

She's meant to stand
for something—revolution,
victory. Liberty

as open air. The rumbling

of starving animals calls out
as polished stone

to sun, unveiling. How sky
pocks with wounds,
our abandon

igniting—how her face mutes
to *perhaps*, to the muscles' tear
our bodies masked with
weightlessness, that illusion

descending. As if
we always knew damage

would carry such light.

URBAN WARFARE AS DESIGN

Four-chambered, the human heart; human lungs
two-winged: the body centers on symmetry

and flux, primary blue flushed
primary red. Add in sun, not as it breaks
through this mosque's shattered ceiling

but colored to a child's
crayoned yolk, and you complete

the wheel, secondaries
only in breakage, scattered tesserae of glass
and tile—amethyst, peach, emerald what remains
of geometry, mosaics'

interlacing circles, triangles crossed to many-rayed stars
because harmony can calm mind

to spirit, because only God
should figure life, because if God
has a face, that brightness can't be drawn

by the fallen, the human hand tumbling
color and glass to spiked flowers and flared wings
in a kaleidoscope's west as if all design

were *spilling*, the body lying inside,
a trip wire; the wrist of the man standing,
a hair trigger. No middle ground, only *cocked*, only *safety*,
all mirrors and fracture, shaken bits

of bright glass. Kaleidoscope, from the Greek: *kalos,*
beautiful, and *eidos,* form. The human shadow

is colorless: the self
ragged at the feet an impetus to the simple
technology of prayer this

moment in rubble, one man cautioning
through the newly blasted entrance, pistol
drawn; one lying flecked
with fallen plaster, stilled

by what may or may not be
his own design. The human heart can be measured
by two human fists. Indigo

into burgundy, the body

flows; gold is what's scrapped, the shaft
of light a helix twisting

between them, shimmering with shreds of paper, Word torn

from syntax, drifting like bits of gold leaf,
like jettisoned ant wings, minute insects born
into flight in summer streetlamps' shining umbrellas

disappeared before morning
into the same blue screen this ceiling now

cracks open to. Light flocks
to the broken. There are no clean lines
to the heart. Even cornered, the torn body zeroes on healing
its own jagged edges, even as the bullet tumbles

from chamber to barrel, repeating the pattern again,
again.

Museum of the Party

To be wicked is to have string at the body's core

but even puppets have eyes and small heels
of polished wood.

At the botched negotiations, the *jungle commando*'s two bodyguards tumbled so
lightly down the mahogany staircase it was as if they'd been surprised
by their own stockinged feet, by what the forest
could polish down to—

How the shrinking canopy of green birds could be muscled
to cry out any name.

     *

Alpha, bravo, Charlie, delta: however you spell the history

of fire, the body is a spool
of cooling wax, an egg balanced on a spoon a girl
might run with toward a field day's finishing line
and a ribbon dyed not winner's red-burning sun, blue-
resisting sky, but the middling yellow she'll collect
again at the science fair, despite how she'll slave
on the paper maché volcano, despite how its mouth
froths on command.

     *

Ambassador to Knee Caps,
Ambassador to Skin, to the first bullets
of rain pitting the dust to pixels
in gray photographs, let us dedicate this museum
by closing the book on pressed faces necessarily torn
to our brightly spotted hunger.

Transparency's a platform. Certain memories must remain
opaque: milky as the delicately veined shell
regretfully cracking, blackened as the weight
of gesture the body clutches even when shoveled
into midnight's shallow soil.

      *

Sun is a yolk severed by glass, by windows hung with yesterday's
elusive weather: ivory cool of morning fog, ivory heat
of afternoon, the room a concave
opalescence resembling only by coincidence
a knucklebone raised after twenty years
from a forest floor of fallen leaves
glossy and sweated with dew,

a bone no larger than the *Bevelhebber*'s cigarette ash
dropped to the polished
mahogany conference table as he raises his shot glass
to surviving confederates, to villages vanished
from a puckered map no longer
taped to a wall where the neighboring sea parched

to small islands. Where a window clears to a day-moon's
dusting, its heel print faint on powder-blue paper.

      *

Ambassador to the Achilles Tendon, Ambassador
to Piano Wire, Cartel of Rain, let this museum once
and for all extinguish the flickering tongues
of teardrops candling our light down
to small pits of shadow. Let us revive
the lost art of periods stamped into heavy letterhead
closing sentences we once blocked in an alphabet
ending in *Uzi*. Let's sand down

the bullet-sprayed brick wall, smooth away its small scars ghosted
with sung-through muscle. Viewed at the proper
angle, the eye socket's scoop is only a small nest
from which a sky-gray egg simply
disappeared overnight, and what does it matter
whose ebony noose uncoiled

*

through the bush where what didn't happen
happened: the American plane dropping south under
its own country's radar to unlock and unload its glittering
not-there cache of AK-47s in a clearing
too narrow for its wings to rescale the forest
in rising, a whole village of men and women
and children directed to hold down the tail
of the small plane which for twelve minutes did
not exist as the pilot-who-wasn't

faced into the sky, gunning the engines to slingshot his way clear
of incident, those impossibly outsized trees.

*

The museum of the party will note in bold: *Even the North
couldn't tilt the jungle to crush us.* The whistle
had blown, the train was going, people, get on:
Ambassadors to Every Door
of the Body, remember each letter
is a hinge, a needle-prick's closed eye from which music
begins in militant beat: *Mi condre tru, mi lobi yu*: remember
that *u*; a single vowel stitched over by *I*, and *collusion*
becomes *collision*:

Remember any name might still be unwritten
from the *us* rostered
beneath bulletproof glass.

*

Ambassador to the Earless Skull, Ambassador
to the Broken Heel, stone nearest that tenderest tongue
of tendon, what the girl, grown now, flexes, anticipating
the starter pistol's pop, feeling the slightest twinge of pain
like the last flutter of distance
in a rainforest bird's call as the trapper nears
with nets and wire and a contract
to export north. A memory not hers but
the weather's, perhaps, the field still steeped
in yesterday's rain riddled by the cleats of some

unfinished match. What can't she see
from this view: forest floors where dusk clocks to lace
bone and earth and absent air, what an electric fan slowly
rotates through displays at a museum
she'll never visit, through shelves of apothecary bottles,
colonial glass dusted and stoppered
with thumbs of new cork, through iron balls and chains
labeled into history as someone
else's failing, the preserved signage of rust insisting
violence is a wand held in outsiders'
long-crumbled hands, not a baton, not the one passed

to her now, mid-race, as she keeps her eye
to the tape of the finishing line and her own
personal best, even as the clouds
above her clear from a day-moon's
smudged fingerprint, a small stain of ash
ground to the boot heel
of some distant, anonymous sky.

ON VENGEANCE

Surfacing starved out the heart
                          of swallowed salt from the kelp's

black bulb, glitter
              a shattering of skin, crystals

clinging to the strand
                  of yarn a child soaks in brine

to replicate the miracle
              of evaporation shimmering in a jelly jar, icy

wick sparking
                   an approximation of winter, close

as you get this far south, the world brief
                                 under glass, yard

a broken abacus, each grass blade beaded
                           with petrified light. Sky

fallen to ice.
That hard flight.

COLONY OF ICE

We struck south to recall winter
as grace, sky no longer constellating

the permanent frost of a country's
baroque sadness, no longer a crystalline breath

purled to whitecaps' lace, froth at the mouth
of the dog wandering the village the morning

that would end her, arrival our single shot
skidding her eyes to that milky glaze

heralding snow, rainforest and thorn desert
gnawed to one echo, a tiny listening

rippling the single sheet we kept unfolding,
the white stare of home.

New Construction

Nothing stops the north drift down, not rising
off-season heat, not bandaged roofs marooning a continent's

storm-gnawed edge, not orange groves ground beneath skeletons
of houses staccatoed with sawdust and wire scrollings

sleeved in *caution*'s seal-sleek skin, the marrow
what electrifies—

        Cadaver by cadaver, the scaffold of bone
breaks down, as a toothpick-thin ship threads

away from its bottle's blown glass—bone
morticians looted and sold: fibula, femur

plied from limbs rag-dolled and rigged
to sheathe plumbing pipes to pass the body

through open-casketed view,
the canal of air rich with lily,

carnation. What's missing
re-circuits into the still-

breathing suspended in a surgical theater three
blinkered states away—

        You can drive all the way to *country*
and never touch earth; you can bottom out

in heartland where vaulted wheat
volts away from the silo's erect

conical tip, harvest
a reversal of light, a flowing-back into the body falling silver

storey by swirling storey, as groundwater
siphoned from arteries tangled in bedrock slips down pipes'

copper-laced throats, southern light streaming
faucet to hose to embedded

flowers along a drive the spreading desert beads
with birdshot—

        Bone by bone, tooth
by tooth, the thorn trees' splintered staircase

sweeps to flame; fist by fist, pulped pines
paper the sky with phantom limb, phantom

needle, so what drills the distance
deeper isn't the question

mark of a dust devil raising a scrim
of spat-up sand and mica wings, but what shivers the blown-

open silence—chaff of the hilltop
dynamited to foundations, to concrete's fluent

stiffening mimicking the shattered
ladder of stone didn't we think would always hold us

up through the whitened
and widening air.

Chemo Session Six

Translucence, organ-soft, bagged on its steel
trident: drip of orphaned light, amber blister

draining to clarity. Healing is the suture
of poison and poison; the body, cups of sand

castled at shoreline. All morning's
a moss creep, orange rust breathing

across winter's bronze face. Sky
is what orbits, sun what stains

the window span with its comet tail
of abandonment: ice so shattered

we swear it fire.

HEALING BY SECONDARY INTENTION

Dark rosette in the lung's

pewter lace, early autumn chill

Splinters of coal

asbestos mist

the long
intention of habit, pack

after pack

Now she is all
effect, and all

coming out at once, the hair she combs
to dogwood and oak-

crisped air—

A dog bite heals by leaving

the palm unstitched, the wound

open

Astringent sky, morning

a feathered arch, quilled light

Summer a lost net
of held rain

Spring, I will find her, all down this street

birds' nests, threaded with silver

TRAPEZE

web-scarabed   the spider's one pupil's black field

brooching night   vacancy

sequined as center   walking-thread and bridged wind   sanctuary a shawl

of piano wire   rosaried rain   cardinal points

mummified flies   sleek skeleton worried to one silk platter

angles light

                                swings

                                                        light-

                        angles platter silk   *one* to worried skeleton

                        sleek flies   mummified points   cardinal

                                        rain   rosaried wire

    piano of shawl a sanctuary   wind-bridged and thread   walking center

            as sequined   vacancy   night-brooching field

                                        black pupils one spiders *the*

                                                scarabed web

Wind Event

Sky through the sweetgum's limbs, powder-blue stasis, thrummed
light: no tornado-heralding downshift

to ivory plum, asparagus cream, the wounded grass of picnics'

deciduous families. No siren: just church bells
marking the hour, silver iced-tea spoons

clattering crystal, fluted clouds
of stirred sugar and lemon; a bird's

tight trill—spine

of a chant, a wing bone's
whistling tunnel: what isn't there, what makes

for flight, the cavity of shadows

hidden in heartwood, the trunk's
detonation to one-hundred-foot tumble

of green light, no

rotation of air, no bullet-spiral just
boom and crack and an arc

of glossed leaves, a shimmering tremor stilling
its veil of dust: ballast and sail—

Ballast, and sail.

Moth Season

Avatars of beige
                    and breakage, Millers would wedge
        between couch cushions, vein accordioned drapes
                              to the pewter the moon cast
off Rocky Mountain foothills our bay window
          angled for: outsized panes, sheer that might have held
              the punched night sky
                         if mimicking hearth wasn't

what made up home. If dusk lamps didn't
                    flash away scape, doubling the living room
                            my father would vanish late nights
                                 with a cut-glass fist
        of amber, the illuminated town
                         strip-mining stars even from the room

he'd darkened, quieting the moths.
Evenings, how they'd bat
        the shades, each lamp the lost
                    lunar shine that had reeled
          them on, when altitude and instinct had woven them
                         a flying carpet rising from tasseled plains
              west, to ladder spring—

Dissolving at *toward*, our hem of timbered rock
                    and prairie grass, house
          of misguided air zeroing out
    crushed-velvet wings to scissored fingers crossed
                         in a wish, in a behind-
                                   the-back lie: powdering
          to the flour dusting my mother's hands, turning

his chicken; my father's long rubbed clean
     of blackboard chalk by the time he'd make it
  home to the thighs and breasts cooling
       on dishwasher-bleached

wedding china, shadowy sprigs
    of pink daisies bordering
  edges chipped the same scallops the wind
       swept sawdust to
     in the corners of half-framed houses
      we neighborhood kids all
    gravitated to
        until the walls
      were sealed, the doors

puzzled in—
    Above tree line, what blooms,
  whorls so slight that, to the survivors
      alighting heads pale
   as matchsticks tipped with white fire in daylight,
     those spoked petals appear
distance itself, portholes in a lit

    and drifting ship. So they remain
  beautiful, baby's breath
    in a bouquet of blighting roses, thorned stems capped
     with blackening ruby capes
    still velvet as alpine air at the needle-
      end of migration—

Light, in nature, is distance
and danger, trigger
to flight. In the night's overflown
volcano—Hawaii, my father's
Navy years, a dusty box
of helicopter-shot slides my sister and I unsecreted to flash
against the closet wall—
flow was a tongue of jeweled fire
spilling toward the flickering
gold ribbon of horizon,
not yet cut off by its own

unfathomable cooling, the years not yet stiffened
to gray pumice, stone weightless
as trampled wings we couldn't
help but grind to ash
in that too-shag carpet
despite all the floated theories how to put down
such suburban risings: '72's
poison mist, '75's water bucket overhung
by one bare lit bulb
calling them home.

EXTINCTION

Each day an emerging
> Ring of rib, definition

Another pearl scimitar
Sheathed in fawn. The paradise of *west* is the sun

Always falling. Nothing's as permanent as passing

Transience, the wing
> Whirred to light, the moon's moth-dust

Ghosting noon. Each blink a little
> *Not-seeing*

Warding off blindness, the gate
> Of skin and lash swings

On its hinges.
How four billion wings must have

Charged the air. Body, ark
> Of extinguished generations, lost

Species, will a little more hunger let her see you
As a rack of rainbows?
> Her last rib spoons each day's

Fainter breath. Migrating air.

Sweet meat of the world
> Picked clean.

Live Performance

Fifteen. World a shell
I held the next day to my ear, future a shore

humming with rock crabs' burgundy palms, all that brilliant
red ink. Day

was afterglow, another childhood

diversion lost: jacks, connect-
the-dots; *Mexican jumping beans*, larvae living off seed-meat

within the flower, *Sebastiana pavoniana*, its
petrifying capsule, until

wings bloom and the long shadow of the body
should nudge open to Baja's

expansive light. In this case,

error. In this case, harvest
for plastic gardens tiered on drugstore counters, a northern

country and no
emergence. Fifteen, my first rock concert: sound pulsed

beyond the body's
capacity for music, so I began to blur what only

slowly grew back as the ocean's roar receded into minute

clarity—pebbles sucked into surf
a tinkling mouthful of polished marbles;

a jostled box of crystal bells, tongues
unhinged. After months

of *jumping* on the forest floor, the larvae should still
to spin a cocoon inside the shell. The shell

should break open. Music
should flow back, the desert birds. The moth should lift

into a sky so electric blue it could hold

the purest disappearance, whatever wings
might write there. The failed ones? The heart

of the flower hardens
around them. The day after, the world

poured back as the glow
ebbed away from those plastic loops we'd

necklaced ourselves with near the monolith, that outsized
speaker, neon dimming to a domestic

Crayola green. A light

went out. The sound
back on: a shell speaking back

the listener; the blood's current, not

the future, that stretch of salt
and pepper sand, rock crabs' rust-red

crackling shells. Eyes, precarious beads

looking back from history. We were waiting for the sky
to lift, for the breath

to unhook. Despite all that light, strobe

and mirror, there was no door
through the music; *dissolve*, what we knocked for—

absence of absence what failed to free.

SPREADING ASH

What's falling isn't her but
September—maple leaves withered
to burnished claws, crushed paper fists
skating across asphalt. She
is a gray arc shimmering

between pines, a winter breath
at summer's end, a small packet

of flung ash. Fired, her limbs' long
ivory wands graveled down——
to beads like sea
glass—cloud white, salmon,
the lime-green patina
bronze breathes—the grains surfacing
finer and grayer, more

like distance, what her eyes fixed
in the end: the window heavy from holding

the lit room after dark; even the woods
inked out, reflection a barrier
to the sputtering stars, glass
a guillotine's silver blade severing light

from the storm blowing in. Absent even her
labored breath, autumn is a golden
serration. All bite
and hollow. How I would

listen for it in her sleep, that burdened
fluency: like a stone skipping
across a lake—two, three,
four times before sinking
somewhere short of the glittering
horizon I first knew

as home, aspens all quavering
quartertones and letting go
branches' bleached ribs;
leaves like tattered
paper lanterns, candlelight fused
to rice paper giving lie
to *burn*, to *dissolve*, as if
that stone were still skipping
beyond my view, sparking
water's skin, autumn's ashen light
all that's ghosting my hands.

Fifteen to Twenty

*Meth—crystal, crank, ice, tweak, glass—the most mind-blowing speed
you can imagine. Was it worth it? Look at me. It was worth everything.*
                                                                    —Anonymous

Scattering the yard's frosted grass, wild onions' emerald tassels
jewel with ice like sea salt, like the tiny translucent year
dangling her cap's golden strands
she, bridging the auditorium stage, clocked
across her forehead, where that night they would tweeze
out windshield glass shattered to grains
of unrefined sugar, to sandpaper grit
smoothing her body's bone cage nearly flush
with world, with that weekend's frame
of battered steel, the Ferris wheel that would lift us
over our downtown stippled with traffic
and street lights, headlights of cruisers still looping

high school's four-block rite. The carnival
of gravity and safety belt crushed the glass vial
she'd palmed from the emergency room
for stash, a quarter ounce packed down
to a single seedless, stemless thumb
imploding in her jeans' pocket
as the guy at the controls, the one who'd
leered at her ass despite her stitched forehead's spray
of spidery black stars, hung us
upside down over the town's

shimmering scalp. At sixteen, I'd smoke anything, risk
that glass lace: she the one holding
to caution those last days before letting go
everything but speed, the crystal that tongued her
to glistening facets flashing
in men's hands like a mirror ball's tossing
sequins of light across a gym floor before the slow
fade-out in a cell whose window
narrowed the sun to less than her waist

twisted sideways. She dumped it all
that night, turning her pocket inside out
over the midway; piped music looped
our glittered spin, and in that tin light
and shimmering jade dust, we were all
sparked surface, all one-
track skin, each brush of breath
or body felt first as the pleasure
of extremity, then too late as *freeze*,

as *burn*. Before any crash, you can't predict
who will swagger away, who will flame
and ash to a few illegible
staccato phrases puffed into sky
long before future's heavy frost and dying-back
suburban yards where wild onions' white knuckles
troll beneath crisp earth and sun
too wintered to warm the last
chrysanthemums lurching after the glow's

fading horizon. Petals
eggshelled with ice fragile as the fallout
that razored her skin: blown windows
from a blast a dozen blocks or a dozen
years away, the night our breath
wasn't quilled with slivered glass and no
crystal ball held the future to such transparency, such

absolute zero. Even her seamless
healed forehead finally embroidered
entirely to mirror work, translucent scales the drug
shivered through her from the char-
black hollow the body begins from and
always surrounds, as if the shattering
cupped in shadow was just her pocket's holding
that night, crushed vial and
a mirror's broken face where her own
might have shone back, given
a little more light.

An Elegiac Tone Predominates

Winter flight
of starlings

dark curtain let fall
across cirrus winged like the gift

of direction
twin lungs charmed

in tin chained at the throat
to spell back breath   a missing

fluency   bloom a freeze
that lasts all season

plastic tulips   roses   graven garden
fully blown that first day given

to undying before the river was born
falling   carving

limestone to canyon over
millions of years

millions what's been scratched
out from history   bronze plaque at the Falls

to stunt distance back to
in the beginning when there was nothing

not horizon
time held in the space

of two hands
this world in parentheses   an aside

beneath a balding
northern sky

hole in the skin   the winding cloth
searchlight zeroing   warming   the body

an amulet   a luminous stem atmosphere
breathes through

Air Hunger

What you hear, barely, the body's
last music: sword

of snow melt, stalactites'

mineral drip. Struggle is what no longer
translates: her sleeping

mouth hung open, the way a snake

unhinges—

Do you remember milk
and vanilla spilled

to fresh snow, how something
so clean had to be so

quickly eaten? Before the food could drift

away from the body
of cold water too clouded to hold

even the face that mothered it
there, into this one

blue bowl.

In case, since you left, you've been wondering,

visiting my mother these terminal days mostly means following
        her shifting commandments how to best rearrange
contents of pink vomit tubs she stacks
        on her hospital bed, fallow ones holding
her smallest belongings: pencils and cracker packets and tiny
        spiral notebooks spooling memos she

increasingly dictates, like the one demanding
        her *right* to vanilla ice cream and chocolate
ice cream and *by god* chocolate-
        vanilla-swirl ice cream, composed when she woke
from five days maximum-dosing morphine in a failed
        bid to die that left her pissed off enough to try

to live again, waking at 2 a.m., channeling
        some orphic voice, *Mother, turn on the breathing light, turn on*
the mother machine, oh god, Mother! Nurses and orderlies
        came running, needles drawn, and what I did was exactly
nothing but think never again will I be able to forget
        the body is a slackening slab of terror

and loneliness, and why
        isn't there a mother machine to never run out
of AA batteries, looping a lullaby to knock
        out this insomnia driving me to television to discover a cross
held to a vampire's washed-out skin sears
        too many films of an earlier generation now lifting
late-night into static like a voice aimed
        at a satellite plummeting (they always say) to

uninhabited sea. *A classic*, meaning—it endures
        repetition? But so does one person's *you don't listen* meaning *I*
don't want to talk and the other's *you never*
        said a thing, meaning, *how*
didn't I hear the night-whisper of scorpions licking the sweet
        flour paste backing the bedroom wallpaper, tails unfurling
like beckoning fingers with her taloned nails, yours
        ticked to the quick from midnight humming the laptop

her name, her name, her name? To my
        best count, her emails included twenty-
seven *sigh*s; *breathless elation*, a baker's dozen; *black boots*, just
        the one spiky pair. My mother's
own divorce anger flared from its thirty-
        year smolder as she pronounced you
dirty bastard, for weeks my own
        personal favorite over her later offerings

of *monster* and *turd*. Maybe
        she's right: the labor of love is not letting it
crush you in its collapse, its uncastled stones
        stringy with moss like in that dream where I was taken
to *a ward of my kind*, which dream-wise meant skeletons
        draped only with their own lost flesh's
lost veins become a seaweed of
        unfathomable agony because strip away everything, cut away
all the body's meat, it will still

        marrow its pain. In the nursing home's sunroom where we
wheel her, my mother calls to order a *staff meeting*, echo
        from her hospital charge-nurse days, outlining
for my sister and I under too-loud Roman numerals and
        capital letters her gripes with the home's
personnel who continue going
        about their tasks unruffled even as she moves
unsuccessfully, hearing
        no second, that the most thoughtless among them be

immediately fired. After all, they're used
            to the hall-hangers, the woman who mantras fourteen hours
of each day *extra, extra, extra*; the one who shakes her thin arms'
            limp fins as she intones every
mundane word in what seemed at first a pitiful
            but later simply an annoying
wavering whine; the woman who asks each passing person, *is it nice
            to eat, can I have some, is it*

good?, repetition clearly no
            indicator of value, more likely just too many words trying
to smother dead space, and too-many-words doesn't
            add up to any meaning at all but ditto
no-words, so why I'm writing this instead of taking down
            my mother's minutes is, first, I would like to offer a friendly
amendment to one of those

            emails, your-her writing *loving you is as natural
as breathing* because if I've learned
            anything watching cancer and emphysema
duking it out in my mother's chest, it's that there's really
            nothing natural about breathing or loving or
letting go; second, who hasn't been someone's

            monster or *turd*? and third, when my mother's ninety-
year-old roommate—fingers too arthritis-gnarled
            to press her call light—asked, *please, could you just
scratch my ear, it's something
            terrible, the itch*, and I bent
down to her as she closed her eyes

            to concentrate the pleasure, I just wanted
to tell you how that faintly furred skin was so
            surprisingly soft, how when she said *thank you, oh, yes, that
is good*, I heard myself reply, *yes,
            oh yes.*

CIRCULATION

                              Longing
extinguished the view, backlit

the body, that trapeze
of scars. *Mother* a sweet diffusion

down the pre-dawn hall. White bird.
Nurse's cap folded

to papery wings.
                    I almost believed

in the wound erased, white towels
cradled in heat, the tweezers' slender

silver wands. The leech she whispered
to the reattached ear's

fresh seam, health
a side effect of hunger, saliva

undamming the blood gifted
with oxygen. Saturated, its work

done, she plucked, flushed
the fat black stitch to the darkened arteries

rooting the city, *flesh*
of my flesh, then nothing but spin.

SWIMMING AT THE Y

The pool's roof is the underskin
of an overpass, concrete ridged like Jersey barriers
lining the road's curve, parentheses to stall

terror at the curb. As if despair doesn't render
any membrane permeable, each lap underscoring

what I'd come to forget: one hour into
my father's six-hour surgery, a nurse guiding me
to a room marked Private Conference and

closing the door. You never touch
bottom, what's always in view: what we'd

dive for, scooping up the quarter he'd toss
the summer I was ten and his heart's leak
only the murmur of distance and late

evening, voices beyond
a bedroom door mooring the child's

drift into sleep. Sinking, the coin's
two silver faces would at once
brighten and blur as his elation at waking

faded with the surgeon's
narration, how he'd held the heart

in his hands, discovered what ultrasound
hadn't: the artery brittle as a cicada husk,
plaque that would shatter

like porcelain if clamped,
my father stroking out as the shards

lodged home. No choice but to close
in damage, to wire
the split breast bone back to hold

one gate fast. How that newly minted valve
must have gleamed

among the scalpels. Retrograde flow,
platelets and foam cells, the heart's
stenosis: I understand

none of it. What I know: this roof
isn't a bridge. The body

is the undertow. The heart is the canary
in the film he loved, sent down to test
the mined air; how she sang, and then

she didn't. The trick was to resist
resurfacing, the body's ache

for return, long enough to trace the wavering
crystalline light to that coin shimmering
ten feet down. How simple to push

air from the lungs, to touch
bottom; how stubborn the body's

capacity for floating. *Aorta* from *to lift,
to heave*, what raises us
to surface: whatever emptiness,

whatever buoyancy.

THE HISTORY OF AIR, PART II

The mimosa folds each tiny rack
of green ribs as the sun

downs and the parking lot grows
more to distance, her night terrors

again coming on as her name
fades from the vomit tub where I inked it as she

did mine on the plastic soap dish I carried
three summers up the mountain to camp, to bonfires and sticky

blackened marshmallows that tasted of
dirt-clotted air—

With all my own
death-fears, what did I

ever know? Not how she'd clutch
the call-light, the narrow snake

and wand of it, its one powder-white eye
to press, wrist watch drifting to her elbow's jut

and sail; not how words would keep waying
up the north road she,

remembering, puts her *should* to, her
hurry to; *Wipe the spoon*, she says, *we will need*

a knife and a fork and a coat where we are going—
Not how I couldn't

let her hand go even as her veins
collapse and she strains

into atmosphere, into the too-thin air
always encircling us.

Cumulative Sentence

Mother of Coughed Blood's Garnet Wings;
Mother of X-rays, of Cat-scans, of *I'm-sorry-*
to-say; Mother of *The-odds-are*, Mother of *Who-can-*
tell, Mother of Chemo, Crystal Pouch and Silver Tree;
Mother of Ambulance White-light, of Alarm-music;
Mother of Breathing Treatments, of Oxygen's Umbilical Tubing;
Mother of Morphine; Mother of Cane, of Walker, of Wheelchair;
Mother of Powdered Rubber Gloves;
Mother of *No*, of *Not-yet*, Mother of Bedside Commodes;
Mother of The Body's Tightening Prison, Mother of
Speed Dial, Mother of Ativan, Mother of Breathing Masks,
of the Flawed Weave of Air; Mother of Hospital Beds, Mother
of Adult Diapers, Mother of *Keep-the-door-open*, of *Don't-leave*; Mother of *Press-*
the-call-light, Mother of *Call 911*; Mother of *No,*
Not Yet; Mother of Graying Grace, Mother of the Pooling
Blood; Mother of Tearing, of *What–time–is–it*,
Mother of Fever and Chill; Mother of *Now*, Mother of Glass
Eyes, Mother of Open Mouth and Filling Lungs;
Mother of the Catheter Bag, of Deepening Topaz, Mother of the Line
of No More; Mother of Bluing Skin, Mother of the Unspooled Heart,
Mother of Flight and Burn, Mother of Cardboard
and Ash, Mother of Smoke, Mother of Air, Mother,
Mother—

ROAD SCATTER

A single vibration breaks the story
to the crystal remnants

of perfect pitch. A wheel-
flung pebble, and sun

pierces the windshield's tint.
The next days

spider the glass. The heart
is damage, a small pit: for *wheel-*

flung pebble, substitute
bullet, and the tire, still

rotating mid-air, catches
the last rayed light: the camera's

pinhole a magnet
for angels, a needle's eye clustered

with crushed wings. Flight
didn't survive the breakage.

What we filmed was landing.

Clearing the House

Now that you exist
only in reverse, in stalled
pixels, stipple

        and field, *never* has lost

its bright teeth: ice-blue stars plummeting
a descent I try
        to read divine.

To count the seasons, bisect the trees:
        winter, summer. Wake, sleep. Trestle

and scar. Time's a series of concentric rings
lacing back to sapling,
        to seed: a dropped stone

unstilling an umber pool. 0s,1s.
Room by room,

        we do as you'd asked: trash
and cull, everything faintly powdered
        with salt ash.

Dying, you seemed to blur outside the lines
        of your body. Empty now,

        the house: there's just
the nothing left, a light through the blinds

we can't shut out.
The illusion of permanence

permanent, it seems: a fading bruise's gold
        stammering the carpet

every morning, whatever direction
         we're turning the key in the lock,
whether or not we turn
as if away.

DENIAL MACHINE

Out my rented window, traffic worries
its one black stitch; a train hums
third-storey floorboards into dream, moon abandoning sea
to newborn stillness. Trench and tide pool
entire. *Within-your-reach*, even the shyest shells
flicker-tease. Indigo
to pearl, ivory spirals, bows
of abalone rain: beauty hinged on tender bodies

ripped away clean. Surface was always
meant for passing. We raid the deep
to believe in *stay*, what I clasp
in your gifted ring, fisting my branded hand
better to glitter
the darkness forward.

FALLING ROCK

No clean getaway, no body
without mirrors: arms
olive and emerald cradle a mountain road's
narrow gray sash, thin to whitecaps
of granite, scrim
of old snow. A name is written
with how many wrong turns?
Disappear, and someone is staged
to unveil the void, *ta-da* the magic cabinet's
spectacular absence, count shadows, sweep the light
spelled to the boards. Someone's left
to haul the smoking valley's wreckage
though the steered-for cliff had promised
the pure dissolve of a plane's
ivory plumage, an immaculate arc
thinning to air. Far
above tarmac, something
worries, loosens. Clouds constellate
sunlight's crumbling mica.
For the moment,
balance, a vigilant pause. No need
for weather: the bluest sky
could tumble it forward.

STILL LIFE WITH MOUSE TORSO AND MINIATURE GRAND PIANO

Hawk-dropped, the body appears first
as abrasion, a bruising of the concrete drive

slight as noon's shadow, as Icarus's falling
through flame and spectacle to the margin
Breughel foregrounded in a sea
of emerald oil.

        At ten, I taught myself to see
only distance; I believed the world scaled

far enough down might narrow
toward grace, the human figured too

outsized to enter. Miniature library, kitchen,

music room: each weekend I'd bevel and stain
and glue: the piano

the finale, dark walnut gloss spanning my hand, lid extended
like a broken wing—

        More *glissando*
than fester, the torso unzips
to an ivory question, spine

levitating free
of its shock of slate fur.

     After a week, barely a gray smudge
mars the driveway's grainy canvas.

        However I had imagined my life
as elaborate as lace, and woven
mostly of air.

No spoil; only vacancy.

Height and length and bend: all curl
to a tiny shepherd's hook, nearing
erasure, insects devouring

                    distance, what seemed
sanctuary, what let God
forget us, perhaps, though most
drought-driven days I just believe in heaven

eternally empty. Cloudless
from here, though the weather

            says rain, an illuminated map
glossing a small shadow's gathering
away from a coast
saw-toothed with fishing villages

                        beneath the radar
homing in on the storm far from earth's shudder

at fault line, the swell
first merely gentling the farthest-out boats
forty-three minutes will surge

to *harbor wave*, the bone-white land
going under.

NEW YEAR

Like stalks of petrified styrofoam, grit
and gray air, fingers of soft coral maroon

by the dozen ashore the splintered stone root
of the lighthouse where I'm climbing

the stepped black spring back
into breathlessness, my mother's ribs cocooning

a shrinking room of furred air; ashen,
limbless, soft corals don't reef, don't branch

into stone but foam the surf
seamlessly, the way forward always

one-half retreat. The coiled stairs
tighten to their finish: a glass torso cool

and vacant with daylight.
From this height, bright cells

barb the sand, beach umbrellas the violet
of her dangled left arm pooling

the body's last heat, the rest of her
grained to pearl. From

this height, the *man of war* bloom
closing the beach is invisible as the tiny families

another day would cluster
beneath the canvas; invisible, the sapphire sails

raised from the fringe of black seaweed
like translucent blue thumbs, the moon jellyfish

washing up among them, pale bells among beach trash,
trailed arms, tiny organs of balance, fine ribs

of vibration ending on this spine of sand I'd come to
to winter the east coast of oblivion, stepping away

from studded tentacles because even the dead
can sting, and I'm trying to gird just one

moment from memory as if each wasn't composed
of the same soft bag of cells, the same transparent eye

absorbing whatever it can and leaving
nothing self behind, not even that flush that slipped

so quickly away *where*, that last
throat-catch then the body

fully coral, the room
salted with distance—No nautilus curl

fossiled in stone, just scattered balloons deflating
among crushed cans and cellophane, everywhere

that tangled trinity: body, poison, air.

O

If *mother* is *alpha* and *omega* spoken
back to the rain, and the most

primitive sound is the human
body beginning and ending in primary
colors, awash red to blue to yellow before the final

returning gray long slapped away for the flush
of birth and crying a clock

set ticking; if, bedridden, she
did believe *cell phone*
could save her, then *comb*, then any word cradling

that sonorous *o*, sound pointing finally
nowhere but into its own

echoing shelter; if her last question wasn't
what? but *what*
what? and zero's the halo

she wears now, *o* become what I had
to leave behind to keep

on going, less than a flicker
of mica in gravel, less than a cicada eye's
translucent pearl bead or a single

faceted grain of sugar spilling
light from the cookie I ate

furtive in her room's corner when she
could no longer swallow and her blood
drained into one arm with

her last words, *Come in*, spoken to the door long
after anyone was knocking.

Last Rites

Darkest where the light begins,
sea I wish myself away to, black silk at sunrise:
from her window, the asphalt world suspends
what remains, a blink of her owlish eyes.

Sea I wish myself away to, black silk at sunrise:
muscle by muscle she abandons her body;
what remains, a blink of her owlish eyes
stalling the future's end to this eternity.

Muscle by muscle, she abandons her body
paused in the skip between two weathers;
stalling the future's end to this eternity
she concentrates, my breath a model for hers

paused in the skip between two weathers.
Believing she'd only forgotten how to breathe,
she concentrates, my breath a model for hers:
in, out—tedious tide before fire's reprieve,

believing she'd only forgotten how to breathe
as her fingers faltered from her piano's keys,
in, out—tedious tide before fire's reprieve,
horizon flaming, her window mute and ashen as she,

as her fingers faltered from her piano's keys
the chaplain held her vacant hand, bone and vein,
horizon flaming her window mute and ashen as she
as he sang her Elvis: "Love Me Tender," "Kentucky Rain."

The chaplain held her vacant hand, bone and vein,
I swear something passed over her eyes, last music
as he sang her Elvis: "Love Me Tender," "Kentucky Rain"—
her voice lost to me, every quaver, each harmonic.

I swear something passed over her eyes, last music;
why hadn't I saved even one syllable?
Her voice lost to me, every quaver, each harmonic—
even a voice mail, what music it would be.

Why hadn't I saved even one syllable?
Her body went on without her two more days;
even a voice mail, what music it would be
now sun's a clot webbed in a world warming and frail.

Her body went on without her two more days,
a porcelain field behind glass, the blue milk sky;
now sun's a clot webbed in a world warming and frail
here in her window, a lighthouse's orphaned eye.

A porcelain field behind glass, the blue milk sky;
I read about the architecture of floating cities, time almost
here; in her window, a lighthouse's orphaned eye
stares vigilance from a distant, drowning coast.

I read about the architecture of floating cities, time almost
to remember her voice before it filled with sand as she
stares vigilance from a distant, drowning coast.
Tell me, where isn't the water rising?

To remember her voice before it filled with sand, as she
from her window, the asphalt world suspends—
tell me, where isn't the water rising
darkest where the light begins.

NOTES

"Museum of the Party": "Bevelhebber" is Dutch for "power head" and was a moniker used to refer to Desi Bouterse, who led a group of fellow noncommissioned army officers in a 1980 coup overthrowing the government of Suriname. Bouterse was the de facto ruler of Suriname through the 1980s, a period of many documented human rights abuses. "Mi condre tru, mi lobi yu" is Sranan Tongo (a Creole language of Suriname) for "My country true, I love you."

"Still Life with Mouse Torso and Miniature Grand Piano": "Harbor wave" is the literal English translation of *tsunami*.